This book is not intended as a substitute for the medical advice of physicians. The reader should regularly consult a physician in matters relating to his/her health and particularly with respect to any symptoms that may require diagnosis or medical attention.

Divine Stationaries

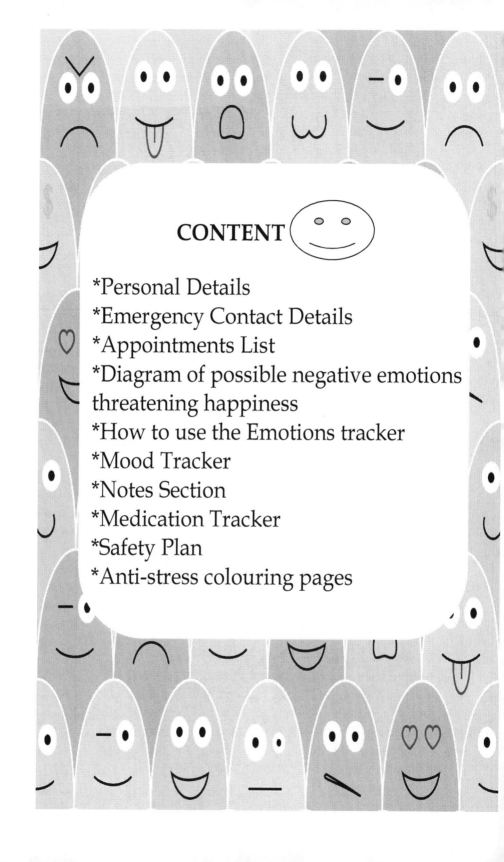

CONTENT

Personal Details

Name:_____

D.O.B:_____

Phone:_____

Email:_____

Health conditions:

_____

_____

_____

_____

_____

_____

My overall mood normally is:

_____

_____

_____

_____

_____

_____

_____

_____

CONTACTS

PSYCHIATRIST/ PSYCHOLOGIST

Name:
Phone:
Email:

NURSE

Name:
Phone:
Email:

LOCAL PHARMACY

Name:
Phone:
Email:

EMERGENCY CONTACTS

CONTACT 1

Name:
Phone:
Email:
Address:

CONTACT 2

Name:
Phone:
Email:
Address:

APPOINTMENTS

For_____ With_____

DATE	TIME	ATTENDED

APPOINTMENTS

For_____ With_____

DATE	TIME	ATTENDED

APPOINTMENTS

For_____ With_____

DATE	TIME	ATTENDED

APPOINTMENTS

For_____ With_____

DATE	TIME	ATTENDED

APPOINTMENTS

For_____   With_____

DATE	TIME	ATTENDED

APPOINTMENTS

For_____ With_____

DATE	TIME	ATTENDED

APPOINTMENTS

For_____ With_____

DATE	TIME	ATTENDED

APPOINTMENTS

For_____   With_____

DATE	TIME	ATTENDED

APPOINTMENTS

For_____ With_____

DATE	TIME	ATTENDED

APPOINTMENTS

For_____   With_____

DATE	TIME	ATTENDED

DESIRE GRATITUDE

PRIDE

POSITIVE EMOTIONS

EUPHORIA

JOY

HOPE

EUPHORIA

EMPATHY HAPPINESS

SENSE OF PURPOSE

RELATIONSHIPS SELF ESTEEM

QUALITY OF LIFE

FRIENDS

HAPPINESS

FAMILY

HEALTH

ATTITUDE

OPTIMISM

SOCIAL INTEREST

FINANCIAL STABILITY

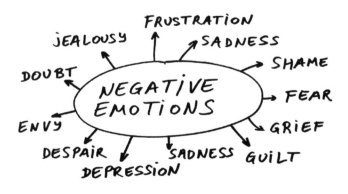

FRUSTRATION

JEALOUSY SADNESS

DOUBT

SHAME

NEGATIVE EMOTIONS

FEAR

ENVY

GRIEF

DESPAIR SADNESS GUILT

DEPRESSION

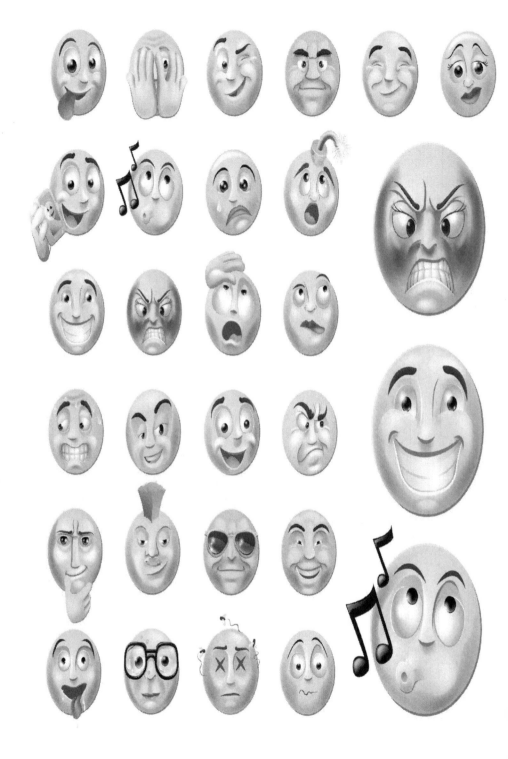

HOW TO USE THIS SECTION:

This section is for you to score your mood throughout the week. Use the scoring system below to chart your daily mood.

Tick which ones applied to you on that day or you can even put the time of day which those feelings occurred.

Use the notes section to write down any particular factors which may have influenced it. Draw pictures of how your feeling, write out your thoughts. How did you get over your negative feelings? This is your own free space to do what you like.

W/C

MON	TUE	WED	THRS	FRIDAY	SAT	SUN
MOOD	MOOD	MOOD	MOOD	MOOD	MOOD	MOOD
☺	☺	☺	☺	☺	☺	☺
WORRIED	WORRIED	WORRIED	WORRIED	WORRIED	WORRIED	WORRIED
TROUBLED	TROUBLED	TROUBLED	TROUBLED	TROUBLED	TROUBLED	TROUBLED
PANIC ATTACKS	PANIC ATTACKS	PANIC ATTACKS	PANIC ATTACKS	PANIC ATTACKS	PANIC ATTACKS	PANIC ATTACKS
SAD	SAD	SAD	SAD	SAD	SAD	SAD
FATIGUE	FATIGUE	FATIGUE	FATIGUE	FATIGUE	FATIGUE	FATIGUE
TEARFUL	TEARFUL	TEARFUL	TEARFUL	TEARFUL	TEARFUL	TEARFUL
TIRED	TIRED	TIRED	TIRED	TIRED	TIRED	TIRED
IRRITATED	IRRITATED	IRRITATED	IRRITATED	IRRITATED	IRRITATED	IRRITATED
HOPELESS	HOPELESS	HOPELESS	HOPELESS	HOPELESS	HOPELESS	HOPELESS
ISOLATED	ISOLATED	ISOLATED	ISOLATED	ISOLATED	ISOLATED	ISOLATED
JOYFUL	JOYFUL	JOYFUL	JOYFUL	JOYFUL	JOYFUL	JOYFUL
ELATED	ELATED	ELATED	ELATED	ELATED	ELATED	ELATED
ENERGIZED	ENERGIZED	ENERGIZED	ENERGIZED	ENERGIZED	ENERGIZED	ENERGIZED
AGGRESSIVE	AGGRESSIVE	AGGRESSIVE	AGGRESSIVE	AGGRESSIVE	AGGRESSIVE	AGGRESSIVE
INSOMNIA	INSOMNIA	INSOMNIA	INSOMNIA	INSOMNIA	INSOMNIA	INSOMNIA

NOTES

MONDAY	
TUESDAY	
WEDNESDAY	
THURSDAY	
FRIDAY	
SATURDAY	
SUNDAY	

W/C

MON	TUE	WED	THRS	FRIDAY	SAT	SUN
MOOD	MOOD	MOOD	MOOD	MOOD	MOOD	MOOD
☺	☺	☺	☺	☺	☺	☺
☹	☹	☹	☹	☹	☹	☹
😮	😮	😮	😮	😮	😮	😮
WORRIED	WORRIED	WORRIED	WORRIED	WORRIED	WORRIED	WORRIED
TROUBLED	TROUBLED	TROUBLED	TROUBLED	TROUBLED	TROUBLED	TROUBLED
PANIC ATTACKS	PANIC ATTACKS	PANIC ATTACKS	PANIC ATTACKS	PANIC ATTACKS	PANIC ATTACKS	PANIC ATTACKS
SAD	SAD	SAD	SAD	SAD	SAD	SAD
FATIGUE	FATIGUE	FATIGUE	FATIGUE	FATIGUE	FATIGUE	FATIGUE
TEARFUL	TEARFUL	TEARFUL	TEARFUL	TEARFUL	TEARFUL	TEARFUL
TIRED	TIRED	TIRED	TIRED	TIRED	TIRED	TIRED
IRRITATED	IRRITATED	IRRITATED	IRRITATED	IRRITATED	IRRITATED	IRRITATED
HOPELESS	HOPELESS	HOPELESS	HOPELESS	HOPELESS	HOPELESS	HOPELESS
ISOLATED	ISOLATED	ISOLATED	ISOLATED	ISOLATED	ISOLATED	ISOLATED
JOYFUL	JOYFUL	JOYFUL	JOYFUL	JOYFUL	JOYFUL	JOYFUL
ELATED	ELATED	ELATED	ELATED	ELATED	ELATED	ELATED
ENERGIZED	ENERGIZED	ENERGIZED	ENERGIZED	ENERGIZED	ENERGIZED	ENERGIZED
AGGRESSIVE	AGGRESSIVE	AGGRESSIVE	AGGRESSIVE	AGGRESSIVE	AGGRESSIVE	AGGRESSIVE
INSOMNIA	INSOMNIA	INSOMNIA	INSOMNIA	INSOMNIA	INSOMNIA	INSOMNIA

NOTES

MONDAY	
TUESDAY	
WEDNESDAY	
THURSDAY	
FRIDAY	
SATURDAY	
SUNDAY	

W/C

MON	TUE	WED	THRS	FRIDAY	SAT	SUN
MOOD	MOOD	MOOD	MOOD	MOOD	MOOD	MOOD
☺ 😐 😕	☺ 😐 😕	☺ 😐 😕	☺ 😐 😕	☺ 😐 😕	☺ 😐 😕	☺ 😐 😕
WORRIED	WORRIED	WORRIED	WORRIED	WORRIED	WORRIED	WORRIED
TROUBLED	TROUBLED	TROUBLED	TROUBLED	TROUBLED	TROUBLED	TROUBLED
PANIC ATTACKS	PANIC ATTACKS	PANIC ATTACKS	PANIC ATTACKS	PANIC ATTACKS	PANIC ATTACKS	PANIC ATTACKS
SAD	SAD	SAD	SAD	SAD	SAD	SAD
FATIGUE	FATIGUE	FATIGUE	FATIGUE	FATIGUE	FATIGUE	FATIGUE
TEARFUL	TEARFUL	TEARFUL	TEARFUL	TEARFUL	TEARFUL	TEARFUL
TIRED	TIRED	TIRED	TIRED	TIRED	TIRED	TIRED
IRRITATED	IRRITATED	IRRITATED	IRRITATED	IRRITATED	IRRITATED	IRRITATED
HOPELESS	HOPELESS	HOPELESS	HOPELESS	HOPELESS	HOPELESS	HOPELESS
ISOLATED	ISOLATED	ISOLATED	ISOLATED	ISOLATED	ISOLATED	ISOLATED
JOYFUL	JOYFUL	JOYFUL	JOYFUL	JOYFUL	JOYFUL	JOYFUL
ELATED	ELATED	ELATED	ELATED	ELATED	ELATED	ELATED
ENERGIZED	ENERGIZED	ENERGIZED	ENERGIZED	ENERGIZED	ENERGIZED	ENERGIZED
AGGRESSIVE	AGGRESSIVE	AGGRESSIVE	AGGRESSIVE	AGGRESSIVE	AGGRESSIVE	AGGRESSIVE
INSOMNIA	INSOMNIA	INSOMNIA	INSOMNIA	INSOMNIA	INSOMNIA	INSOMNIA

NOTES

MONDAY	
TUESDAY	
WEDNESDAY	
THURSDAY	
FRIDAY	
SATURDAY	
SUNDAY	

W/C

MON	TUE	WED	THRS	FRIDAY	SAT	SUN
MOOD	MOOD	MOOD	MOOD	MOOD	MOOD	MOOD
😊 😐 😞	😊 😐 😞	😊 😐 😞	😊 😐 😞	😊 😐 😞	😊 😐 😞	😊 😐 😞
WORRIED	WORRIED	WORRIED	WORRIED	WORRIED	WORRIED	WORRIED
TROUBLED	TROUBLED	TROUBLED	TROUBLED	TROUBLED	TROUBLED	TROUBLED
PANIC ATTACKS	PANIC ATTACKS	PANIC ATTACKS	PANIC ATTACKS	PANIC ATTACKS	PANIC ATTACKS	PANIC ATTACKS
SAD	SAD	SAD	SAD	SAD	SAD	SAD
FATIGUE	FATIGUE	FATIGUE	FATIGUE	FATIGUE	FATIGUE	FATIGUE
TEARFUL	TEARFUL	TEARFUL	TEARFUL	TEARFUL	TEARFUL	TEARFUL
TIRED	TIRED	TIRED	TIRED	TIRED	TIRED	TIRED
IRRITATED	IRRITATED	IRRITATED	IRRITATED	IRRITATED	IRRITATED	IRRITATED
HOPELESS	HOPELESS	HOPELESS	HOPELESS	HOPELESS	HOPELESS	HOPELESS
ISOLATED	ISOLATED	ISOLATED	ISOLATED	ISOLATED	ISOLATED	ISOLATED
JOYFUL	JOYFUL	JOYFUL	JOYFUL	JOYFUL	JOYFUL	JOYFUL
ELATED	ELATED	ELATED	ELATED	ELATED	ELATED	ELATED
ENERGIZED	ENERGIZED	ENERGIZED	ENERGIZED	ENERGIZED	ENERGIZED	ENERGIZED
AGGRESSIVE	AGGRESSIVE	AGGRESSIVE	AGGRESSIVE	AGGRESSIVE	AGGRESSIVE	AGGRESSIVE
INSOMNIA	INSOMNIA	INSOMNIA	INSOMNIA	INSOMNIA	INSOMNIA	INSOMNIA

NOTES

MONDAY	TUESDAY	WEDNESDAY	THURSDAY	FRIDAY	SATURDAY	SUNDAY

W/C

MON	TUE	WED	THRS	FRIDAY	SAT	SUN
MOOD	MOOD	MOOD	MOOD	MOOD	MOOD	MOOD
☺ ☹ 😐	☺ ☹ 😐	☺ ☹ 😐	☺ ☹ 😐	☺ ☹ 😐	☺ ☹ 😐	☺ ☹ 😐
WORRIED	WORRIED	WORRIED	WORRIED	WORRIED	WORRIED	WORRIED
TROUBLED	TROUBLED	TROUBLED	TROUBLED	TROUBLED	TROUBLED	TROUBLED
PANIC ATTACKS	PANIC ATTACKS	PANIC ATTACKS	PANIC ATTACKS	PANIC ATTACKS	PANIC ATTACKS	PANIC ATTACKS
SAD	SAD	SAD	SAD	SAD	SAD	SAD
FATIGUE	FATIGUE	FATIGUE	FATIGUE	FATIGUE	FATIGUE	FATIGUE
TEARFUL	TEARFUL	TEARFUL	TEARFUL	TEARFUL	TEARFUL	TEARFUL
TIRED	TIRED	TIRED	TIRED	TIRED	TIRED	TIRED
IRRITATED	IRRITATED	IRRITATED	IRRITATED	IRRITATED	IRRITATED	IRRITATED
HOPELESS	HOPELESS	HOPELESS	HOPELESS	HOPELESS	HOPELESS	HOPELESS
ISOLATED	ISOLATED	ISOLATED	ISOLATED	ISOLATED	ISOLATED	ISOLATED
JOYFUL	JOYFUL	JOYFUL	JOYFUL	JOYFUL	JOYFUL	JOYFUL
ELATED	ELATED	ELATED	ELATED	ELATED	ELATED	ELATED
ENERGIZED	ENERGIZED	ENERGIZED	ENERGIZED	ENERGIZED	ENERGIZED	ENERGIZED
AGGRESSIVE	AGGRESSIVE	AGGRESSIVE	AGGRESSIVE	AGGRESSIVE	AGGRESSIVE	AGGRESSIVE
INSOMNIA	INSOMNIA	INSOMNIA	INSOMNIA	INSOMNIA	INSOMNIA	INSOMNIA

NOTES

MONDAY	
TUESDAY	
WEDNESDAY	
THURSDAY	
FRIDAY	
SATURDAY	
SUNDAY	

W/C

MON	TUE	WED	THRS	FRIDAY	SAT	SUN
MOOD	MOOD	MOOD	MOOD	MOOD	MOOD	MOOD
🙂 😐 ☹️	🙂 😐 ☹️	🙂 😐 ☹️	🙂 😐 ☹️	🙂 😐 ☹️	🙂 😐 ☹️	🙂 😐 ☹️
WORRIED	WORRIED	WORRIED	WORRIED	WORRIED	WORRIED	WORRIED
TROUBLED	TROUBLED	TROUBLED	TROUBLED	TROUBLED	TROUBLED	TROUBLED
PANIC ATTACKS	PANIC ATTACKS	PANIC ATTACKS	PANIC ATTACKS	PANIC ATTACKS	PANIC ATTACKS	PANIC ATTACKS
SAD	SAD	SAD	SAD	SAD	SAD	SAD
FATIGUE	FATIGUE	FATIGUE	FATIGUE	FATIGUE	FATIGUE	FATIGUE
TEARFUL	TEARFUL	TEARFUL	TEARFUL	TEARFUL	TEARFUL	TEARFUL
TIRED	TIRED	TIRED	TIRED	TIRED	TIRED	TIRED
IRRITATED	IRRITATED	IRRITATED	IRRITATED	IRRITATED	IRRITATED	IRRITATED
HOPELESS	HOPELESS	HOPELESS	HOPELESS	HOPELESS	HOPELESS	HOPELESS
ISOLATED	ISOLATED	ISOLATED	ISOLATED	ISOLATED	ISOLATED	ISOLATED
JOYFUL	JOYFUL	JOYFUL	JOYFUL	JOYFUL	JOYFUL	JOYFUL
ELATED	ELATED	ELATED	ELATED	ELATED	ELATED	ELATED
ENERGIZED	ENERGIZED	ENERGIZED	ENERGIZED	ENERGIZED	ENERGIZED	ENERGIZED
AGGRESSIVE	AGGRESSIVE	AGGRESSIVE	AGGRESSIVE	AGGRESSIVE	AGGRESSIVE	AGGRESSIVE
INSOMNIA	INSOMNIA	INSOMNIA	INSOMNIA	INSOMNIA	INSOMNIA	INSOMNIA

NOTES

MONDAY	
TUESDAY	
WEDNESDAY	
THURSDAY	
FRIDAY	
SATURDAY	
SUNDAY	

W/C

MON	TUE	WED	THRS	FRIDAY	SAT	SUN
MOOD	MOOD	MOOD	MOOD	MOOD	MOOD	MOOD
☺ ☹ 😐	☺ ☹ 😐	☺ ☹ 😐	☺ ☹ 😐	☺ ☹ 😐	☺ ☹ 😐	☺ ☹ 😐
WORRIED	WORRIED	WORRIED	WORRIED	WORRIED	WORRIED	WORRIED
TROUBLED	TROUBLED	TROUBLED	TROUBLED	TROUBLED	TROUBLED	TROUBLED
PANIC ATTACKS	PANIC ATTACKS	PANIC ATTACKS	PANIC ATTACKS	PANIC ATTACKS	PANIC ATTACKS	PANIC ATTACKS
SAD	SAD	SAD	SAD	SAD	SAD	SAD
FATIGUE	FATIGUE	FATIGUE	FATIGUE	FATIGUE	FATIGUE	FATIGUE
TEARFUL	TEARFUL	TEARFUL	TEARFUL	TEARFUL	TEARFUL	TEARFUL
TIRED	TIRED	TIRED	TIRED	TIRED	TIRED	TIRED
IRRITATED	IRRITATED	IRRITATED	IRRITATED	IRRITATED	IRRITATED	IRRITATED
HOPELESS	HOPELESS	HOPELESS	HOPELESS	HOPELESS	HOPELESS	HOPELESS
ISOLATED	ISOLATED	ISOLATED	ISOLATED	ISOLATED	ISOLATED	ISOLATED
JOYFUL	JOYFUL	JOYFUL	JOYFUL	JOYFUL	JOYFUL	JOYFUL
ELATED	ELATED	ELATED	ELATED	ELATED	ELATED	ELATED
ENERGIZED	ENERGIZED	ENERGIZED	ENERGIZED	ENERGIZED	ENERGIZED	ENERGIZED
AGGRESSIVE	AGGRESSIVE	AGGRESSIVE	AGGRESSIVE	AGGRESSIVE	AGGRESSIVE	AGGRESSIVE
INSOMNIA	INSOMNIA	INSOMNIA	INSOMNIA	INSOMNIA	INSOMNIA	INSOMNIA

NOTES

MONDAY	
TUESDAY	
WEDNESDAY	
THURSDAY	
FRIDAY	
SATURDAY	
SUNDAY	

W/C

MON	TUE	WED	THRS	FRIDAY	SAT	SUN
MOOD	MOOD	MOOD	MOOD	MOOD	MOOD	MOOD
😊 🙁 😐	😊 🙁 😐	😊 🙁 😐	😊 🙁 😐	😊 🙁 😐	😊 🙁 😐	😊 🙁 😐
WORRIED	WORRIED	WORRIED	WORRIED	WORRIED	WORRIED	WORRIED
TROUBLED	TROUBLED	TROUBLED	TROUBLED	TROUBLED	TROUBLED	TROUBLED
PANIC ATTACKS	PANIC ATTACKS	PANIC ATTACKS	PANIC ATTACKS	PANIC ATTACKS	PANIC ATTACKS	PANIC ATTACKS
SAD	SAD	SAD	SAD	SAD	SAD	SAD
FATIGUE	FATIGUE	FATIGUE	FATIGUE	FATIGUE	FATIGUE	FATIGUE
TEARFUL	TEARFUL	TEARFUL	TEARFUL	TEARFUL	TEARFUL	TEARFUL
TIRED	TIRED	TIRED	TIRED	TIRED	TIRED	TIRED
IRRITATED	IRRITATED	IRRITATED	IRRITATED	IRRITATED	IRRITATED	IRRITATED
HOPELESS	HOPELESS	HOPELESS	HOPELESS	HOPELESS	HOPELESS	HOPELESS
ISOLATED	ISOLATED	ISOLATED	ISOLATED	ISOLATED	ISOLATED	ISOLATED
JOYFUL	JOYFUL	JOYFUL	JOYFUL	JOYFUL	JOYFUL	JOYFUL
ELATED	ELATED	ELATED	ELATED	ELATED	ELATED	ELATED
ENERGIZED	ENERGIZED	ENERGIZED	ENERGIZED	ENERGIZED	ENERGIZED	ENERGIZED
AGGRESSIVE	AGGRESSIVE	AGGRESSIVE	AGGRESSIVE	AGGRESSIVE	AGGRESSIVE	AGGRESSIVE
INSOMNIA	INSOMNIA	INSOMNIA	INSOMNIA	INSOMNIA	INSOMNIA	INSOMNIA

NOTES

MONDAY	
TUESDAY	
WEDNESDAY	
THURSDAY	
FRIDAY	
SATURDAY	
SUNDAY	

W/C

MON	TUE	WED	THRS	FRIDAY	SAT	SUN
MOOD	MOOD	MOOD	MOOD	MOOD	MOOD	MOOD
☺ 😐 🙁	☺ 😐 🙁	☺ 😐 🙁	☺ 😐 🙁	☺ 😐 🙁	☺ 😐 🙁	☺ 😐 🙁
WORRIED	WORRIED	WORRIED	WORRIED	WORRIED	WORRIED	WORRIED
TROUBLED	TROUBLED	TROUBLED	TROUBLED	TROUBLED	TROUBLED	TROUBLED
PANIC ATTACKS	PANIC ATTACKS	PANIC ATTACKS	PANIC ATTACKS	PANIC ATTACKS	PANIC ATTACKS	PANIC ATTACKS
SAD	SAD	SAD	SAD	SAD	SAD	SAD
FATIGUE	FATIGUE	FATIGUE	FATIGUE	FATIGUE	FATIGUE	FATIGUE
TEARFUL	TEARFUL	TEARFUL	TEARFUL	TEARFUL	TEARFUL	TEARFUL
TIRED	TIRED	TIRED	TIRED	TIRED	TIRED	TIRED
IRRITATED	IRRITATED	IRRITATED	IRRITATED	IRRITATED	IRRITATED	IRRITATED
HOPELESS	HOPELESS	HOPELESS	HOPELESS	HOPELESS	HOPELESS	HOPELESS
ISOLATED	ISOLATED	ISOLATED	ISOLATED	ISOLATED	ISOLATED	ISOLATED
JOYFUL	JOYFUL	JOYFUL	JOYFUL	JOYFUL	JOYFUL	JOYFUL
ELATED	ELATED	ELATED	ELATED	ELATED	ELATED	ELATED
ENERGIZED	ENERGIZED	ENERGIZED	ENERGIZED	ENERGIZED	ENERGIZED	ENERGIZED
AGGRESSIVE	AGGRESSIVE	AGGRESSIVE	AGGRESSIVE	AGGRESSIVE	AGGRESSIVE	AGGRESSIVE
INSOMNIA	INSOMNIA	INSOMNIA	INSOMNIA	INSOMNIA	INSOMNIA	INSOMNIA

NOTES

	MONDAY	
	TUESDAY	
	WEDNESDAY	
	THURSDAY	
	FRIDAY	
	SATURDAY	
	SUNDAY	

W/C

MON	TUE	WED	THRS	FRIDAY	SAT	SUN
MOOD	MOOD	MOOD	MOOD	MOOD	MOOD	MOOD
😊 😐 😟	😊 😐 😟	😊 😐 😟	😊 😐 😟	😊 😐 😟	😊 😐 😟	😊 😐 😟
WORRIED	WORRIED	WORRIED	WORRIED	WORRIED	WORRIED	WORRIED
TROUBLED	TROUBLED	TROUBLED	TROUBLED	TROUBLED	TROUBLED	TROUBLED
PANIC ATTACKS	PANIC ATTACKS	PANIC ATTACKS	PANIC ATTACKS	PANIC ATTACKS	PANIC ATTACKS	PANIC ATTACKS
SAD	SAD	SAD	SAD	SAD	SAD	SAD
FATIGUE	FATIGUE	FATIGUE	FATIGUE	FATIGUE	FATIGUE	FATIGUE
TEARFUL	TEARFUL	TEARFUL	TEARFUL	TEARFUL	TEARFUL	TEARFUL
TIRED	TIRED	TIRED	TIRED	TIRED	TIRED	TIRED
IRRITATED	IRRITATED	IRRITATED	IRRITATED	IRRITATED	IRRITATED	IRRITATED
HOPELESS	HOPELESS	HOPELESS	HOPELESS	HOPELESS	HOPELESS	HOPELESS
ISOLATED	ISOLATED	ISOLATED	ISOLATED	ISOLATED	ISOLATED	ISOLATED
JOYFUL	JOYFUL	JOYFUL	JOYFUL	JOYFUL	JOYFUL	JOYFUL
ELATED	ELATED	ELATED	ELATED	ELATED	ELATED	ELATED
ENERGIZED	ENERGIZED	ENERGIZED	ENERGIZED	ENERGIZED	ENERGIZED	ENERGIZED
AGGRESSIVE	AGGRESSIVE	AGGRESSIVE	AGGRESSIVE	AGGRESSIVE	AGGRESSIVE	AGGRESSIVE
INSOMNIA	INSOMNIA	INSOMNIA	INSOMNIA	INSOMNIA	INSOMNIA	INSOMNIA

NOTES

MONDAY	
TUESDAY	
WEDNESDAY	
THURSDAY	
FRIDAY	
SATURDAY	
SUNDAY	

W/C

MON	TUE	WED	THRS	FRIDAY	SAT	SUN
MOOD	MOOD	MOOD	MOOD	MOOD	MOOD	MOOD
☺	☺	☺	☺	☺	☺	☺
WORRIED	WORRIED	WORRIED	WORRIED	WORRIED	WORRIED	WORRIED
TROUBLED	TROUBLED	TROUBLED	TROUBLED	TROUBLED	TROUBLED	TROUBLED
PANIC ATTACKS	PANIC ATTACKS	PANIC ATTACKS	PANIC ATTACKS	PANIC ATTACKS	PANIC ATTACKS	PANIC ATTACKS
SAD	SAD	SAD	SAD	SAD	SAD	SAD
FATIGUE	FATIGUE	FATIGUE	FATIGUE	FATIGUE	FATIGUE	FATIGUE
TEARFUL	TEARFUL	TEARFUL	TEARFUL	TEARFUL	TEARFUL	TEARFUL
TIRED	TIRED	TIRED	TIRED	TIRED	TIRED	TIRED
IRRITATED	IRRITATED	IRRITATED	IRRITATED	IRRITATED	IRRITATED	IRRITATED
HOPELESS	HOPELESS	HOPELESS	HOPELESS	HOPELESS	HOPELESS	HOPELESS
ISOLATED	ISOLATED	ISOLATED	ISOLATED	ISOLATED	ISOLATED	ISOLATED
JOYFUL	JOYFUL	JOYFUL	JOYFUL	JOYFUL	JOYFUL	JOYFUL
ELATED	ELATED	ELATED	ELATED	ELATED	ELATED	ELATED
ENERGIZED	ENERGIZED	ENERGIZED	ENERGIZED	ENERGIZED	ENERGIZED	ENERGIZED
AGGRESSIVE	AGGRESSIVE	AGGRESSIVE	AGGRESSIVE	AGGRESSIVE	AGGRESSIVE	AGGRESSIVE
INSOMNIA	INSOMNIA	INSOMNIA	INSOMNIA	INSOMNIA	INSOMNIA	INSOMNIA

NOTES

MONDAY	TUESDAY	WEDNESDAY	THURSDAY	FRIDAY	SATURDAY	SUNDAY

W/C

MON	TUE	WED	THRS	FRIDAY	SAT	SUN
MOOD	MOOD	MOOD	MOOD	MOOD	MOOD	MOOD
☺ ☹	☺ ☹	☺ ☹	☺ ☹	☺ ☹	☺ ☹	☺ ☹
WORRIED	WORRIED	WORRIED	WORRIED	WORRIED	WORRIED	WORRIED
TROUBLED	TROUBLED	TROUBLED	TROUBLED	TROUBLED	TROUBLED	TROUBLED
PANIC ATTACKS	PANIC ATTACKS	PANIC ATTACKS	PANIC ATTACKS	PANIC ATTACKS	PANIC ATTACKS	PANIC ATTACKS
SAD	SAD	SAD	SAD	SAD	SAD	SAD
FATIGUE	FATIGUE	FATIGUE	FATIGUE	FATIGUE	FATIGUE	FATIGUE
TEARFUL	TEARFUL	TEARFUL	TEARFUL	TEARFUL	TEARFUL	TEARFUL
TIRED	TIRED	TIRED	TIRED	TIRED	TIRED	TIRED
IRRITATED	IRRITATED	IRRITATED	IRRITATED	IRRITATED	IRRITATED	IRRITATED
HOPELESS	HOPELESS	HOPELESS	HOPELESS	HOPELESS	HOPELESS	HOPELESS
ISOLATED	ISOLATED	ISOLATED	ISOLATED	ISOLATED	ISOLATED	ISOLATED
JOYFUL	JOYFUL	JOYFUL	JOYFUL	JOYFUL	JOYFUL	JOYFUL
ELATED	ELATED	ELATED	ELATED	ELATED	ELATED	ELATED
ENERGIZED	ENERGIZED	ENERGIZED	ENERGIZED	ENERGIZED	ENERGIZED	ENERGIZED
AGGRESSIVE	AGGRESSIVE	AGGRESSIVE	AGGRESSIVE	AGGRESSIVE	AGGRESSIVE	AGGRESSIVE
INSOMNIA	INSOMNIA	INSOMNIA	INSOMNIA	INSOMNIA	INSOMNIA	INSOMNIA

NOTES

MONDAY	
TUESDAY	
WEDNESDAY	
THURSDAY	
FRIDAY	
SATURDAY	
SUNDAY	

W/C

MON	TUE	WED	THRS	FRIDAY	SAT	SUN
MOOD	MOOD	MOOD	MOOD	MOOD	MOOD	MOOD
☺ 😐 🙁	☺ 😐 🙁	☺ 😐 🙁	☺ 😐 🙁	☺ 😐 🙁	☺ 😐 🙁	☺ 😐 🙁
WORRIED	WORRIED	WORRIED	WORRIED	WORRIED	WORRIED	WORRIED
TROUBLED	TROUBLED	TROUBLED	TROUBLED	TROUBLED	TROUBLED	TROUBLED
PANIC ATTACKS	PANIC ATTACKS	PANIC ATTACKS	PANIC ATTACKS	PANIC ATTACKS	PANIC ATTACKS	PANIC ATTACKS
SAD	SAD	SAD	SAD	SAD	SAD	SAD
FATIGUE	FATIGUE	FATIGUE	FATIGUE	FATIGUE	FATIGUE	FATIGUE
TEARFUL	TEARFUL	TEARFUL	TEARFUL	TEARFUL	TEARFUL	TEARFUL
TIRED	TIRED	TIRED	TIRED	TIRED	TIRED	TIRED
IRRITATED	IRRITATED	IRRITATED	IRRITATED	IRRITATED	IRRITATED	IRRITATED
HOPELESS	HOPELESS	HOPELESS	HOPELESS	HOPELESS	HOPELESS	HOPELESS
ISOLATED	ISOLATED	ISOLATED	ISOLATED	ISOLATED	ISOLATED	ISOLATED
JOYFUL	JOYFUL	JOYFUL	JOYFUL	JOYFUL	JOYFUL	JOYFUL
ELATED	ELATED	ELATED	ELATED	ELATED	ELATED	ELATED
ENERGIZED	ENERGIZED	ENERGIZED	ENERGIZED	ENERGIZED	ENERGIZED	ENERGIZED
AGGRESSIVE	AGGRESSIVE	AGGRESSIVE	AGGRESSIVE	AGGRESSIVE	AGGRESSIVE	AGGRESSIVE
INSOMNIA	INSOMNIA	INSOMNIA	INSOMNIA	INSOMNIA	INSOMNIA	INSOMNIA

NOTES

MONDAY	
TUESDAY	
WEDNESDAY	
THURSDAY	
FRIDAY	
SATURDAY	
SUNDAY	

W/C

MON	TUE	WED	THRS	FRIDAY	SAT	SUN
MOOD	MOOD	MOOD	MOOD	MOOD	MOOD	MOOD
☺ ☹ 😐	☺ ☹ 😐	☺ ☹ 😐	☺ ☹ 😐	☺ ☹ 😐	☺ ☹ 😐	☺ ☹ 😐
WORRIED	WORRIED	WORRIED	WORRIED	WORRIED	WORRIED	WORRIED
TROUBLED	TROUBLED	TROUBLED	TROUBLED	TROUBLED	TROUBLED	TROUBLED
PANIC ATTACKS	PANIC ATTACKS	PANIC ATTACKS	PANIC ATTACKS	PANIC ATTACKS	PANIC ATTACKS	PANIC ATTACKS
SAD	SAD	SAD	SAD	SAD	SAD	SAD
FATIGUE	FATIGUE	FATIGUE	FATIGUE	FATIGUE	FATIGUE	FATIGUE
TEARFUL	TEARFUL	TEARFUL	TEARFUL	TEARFUL	TEARFUL	TEARFUL
TIRED	TIRED	TIRED	TIRED	TIRED	TIRED	TIRED
IRRITATED	IRRITATED	IRRITATED	IRRITATED	IRRITATED	IRRITATED	IRRITATED
HOPELESS	HOPELESS	HOPELESS	HOPELESS	HOPELESS	HOPELESS	HOPELESS
ISOLATED	ISOLATED	ISOLATED	ISOLATED	ISOLATED	ISOLATED	ISOLATED
JOYFUL	JOYFUL	JOYFUL	JOYFUL	JOYFUL	JOYFUL	JOYFUL
ELATED	ELATED	ELATED	ELATED	ELATED	ELATED	ELATED
ENERGIZED	ENERGIZED	ENERGIZED	ENERGIZED	ENERGIZED	ENERGIZED	ENERGIZED
AGGRESSIVE	AGGRESSIVE	AGGRESSIVE	AGGRESSIVE	AGGRESSIVE	AGGRESSIVE	AGGRESSIVE
INSOMNIA	INSOMNIA	INSOMNIA	INSOMNIA	INSOMNIA	INSOMNIA	INSOMNIA

NOTES

MONDAY	
TUESDAY	
WEDNESDAY	
THURSDAY	
FRIDAY	
SATURDAY	
SUNDAY	

W/C

MON	TUE	WED	THRS	FRIDAY	SAT	SUN
MOOD	MOOD	MOOD	MOOD	MOOD	MOOD	MOOD
☺ 😐 😟	☺ 😐 😟	☺ 😐 😟	☺ 😐 😟	☺ 😐 😟	☺ 😐 😟	☺ 😐 😟
WORRIED	WORRIED	WORRIED	WORRIED	WORRIED	WORRIED	WORRIED
TROUBLED	TROUBLED	TROUBLED	TROUBLED	TROUBLED	TROUBLED	TROUBLED
PANIC ATTACKS	PANIC ATTACKS	PANIC ATTACKS	PANIC ATTACKS	PANIC ATTACKS	PANIC ATTACKS	PANIC ATTACKS
SAD	SAD	SAD	SAD	SAD	SAD	SAD
FATIGUE	FATIGUE	FATIGUE	FATIGUE	FATIGUE	FATIGUE	FATIGUE
TEARFUL	TEARFUL	TEARFUL	TEARFUL	TEARFUL	TEARFUL	TEARFUL
TIRED	TIRED	TIRED	TIRED	TIRED	TIRED	TIRED
IRRITATED	IRRITATED	IRRITATED	IRRITATED	IRRITATED	IRRITATED	IRRITATED
HOPELESS	HOPELESS	HOPELESS	HOPELESS	HOPELESS	HOPELESS	HOPELESS
ISOLATED	ISOLATED	ISOLATED	ISOLATED	ISOLATED	ISOLATED	ISOLATED
JOYFUL	JOYFUL	JOYFUL	JOYFUL	JOYFUL	JOYFUL	JOYFUL
ELATED	ELATED	ELATED	ELATED	ELATED	ELATED	ELATED
ENERGIZED	ENERGIZED	ENERGIZED	ENERGIZED	ENERGIZED	ENERGIZED	ENERGIZED
AGGRESSIVE	AGGRESSIVE	AGGRESSIVE	AGGRESSIVE	AGGRESSIVE	AGGRESSIVE	AGGRESSIVE
INSOMNIA	INSOMNIA	INSOMNIA	INSOMNIA	INSOMNIA	INSOMNIA	INSOMNIA

NOTES

MONDAY	
TUESDAY	
WEDNESDAY	
THURSDAY	
FRIDAY	
SATURDAY	
SUNDAY	

W/C

MON	TUE	WED	THRS	FRIDAY	SAT	SUN
MOOD	MOOD	MOOD	MOOD	MOOD	MOOD	MOOD
☺ ☹ 😐	☺ ☹ 😐	☺ ☹ 😐	☺ ☹ 😐	☺ ☹ 😐	☺ ☹ 😐	☺ ☹ 😐
WORRIED	WORRIED	WORRIED	WORRIED	WORRIED	WORRIED	WORRIED
TROUBLED	TROUBLED	TROUBLED	TROUBLED	TROUBLED	TROUBLED	TROUBLED
PANIC ATTACKS	PANIC ATTACKS	PANIC ATTACKS	PANIC ATTACKS	PANIC ATTACKS	PANIC ATTACKS	PANIC ATTACKS
SAD	SAD	SAD	SAD	SAD	SAD	SAD
FATIGUE	FATIGUE	FATIGUE	FATIGUE	FATIGUE	FATIGUE	FATIGUE
TEARFUL	TEARFUL	TEARFUL	TEARFUL	TEARFUL	TEARFUL	TEARFUL
TIRED	TIRED	TIRED	TIRED	TIRED	TIRED	TIRED
IRRITATED	IRRITATED	IRRITATED	IRRITATED	IRRITATED	IRRITATED	IRRITATED
HOPELESS	HOPELESS	HOPELESS	HOPELESS	HOPELESS	HOPELESS	HOPELESS
ISOLATED	ISOLATED	ISOLATED	ISOLATED	ISOLATED	ISOLATED	ISOLATED
JOYFUL	JOYFUL	JOYFUL	JOYFUL	JOYFUL	JOYFUL	JOYFUL
ELATED	ELATED	ELATED	ELATED	ELATED	ELATED	ELATED
ENERGIZED	ENERGIZED	ENERGIZED	ENERGIZED	ENERGIZED	ENERGIZED	ENERGIZED
AGGRESSIVE	AGGRESSIVE	AGGRESSIVE	AGGRESSIVE	AGGRESSIVE	AGGRESSIVE	AGGRESSIVE
INSOMNIA	INSOMNIA	INSOMNIA	INSOMNIA	INSOMNIA	INSOMNIA	INSOMNIA

NOTES

MONDAY	
TUESDAY	
WEDNESDAY	
THURSDAY	
FRIDAY	
SATURDAY	
SUNDAY	

W/C

MON	TUE	WED	THRS	FRIDAY	SAT	SUN
MOOD	MOOD	MOOD	MOOD	MOOD	MOOD	MOOD
☺ ☹ 😐	☺ ☹ 😐	☺ ☹ 😐	☺ ☹ 😐	☺ ☹ 😐	☺ ☹ 😐	☺ ☹ 😐
WORRIED	WORRIED	WORRIED	WORRIED	WORRIED	WORRIED	WORRIED
TROUBLED	TROUBLED	TROUBLED	TROUBLED	TROUBLED	TROUBLED	TROUBLED
PANIC ATTACKS	PANIC ATTACKS	PANIC ATTACKS	PANIC ATTACKS	PANIC ATTACKS	PANIC ATTACKS	PANIC ATTACKS
SAD	SAD	SAD	SAD	SAD	SAD	SAD
FATIGUE	FATIGUE	FATIGUE	FATIGUE	FATIGUE	FATIGUE	FATIGUE
TEARFUL	TEARFUL	TEARFUL	TEARFUL	TEARFUL	TEARFUL	TEARFUL
TIRED	TIRED	TIRED	TIRED	TIRED	TIRED	TIRED
IRRITATED	IRRITATED	IRRITATED	IRRITATED	IRRITATED	IRRITATED	IRRITATED
HOPELESS	HOPELESS	HOPELESS	HOPELESS	HOPELESS	HOPELESS	HOPELESS
ISOLATED	ISOLATED	ISOLATED	ISOLATED	ISOLATED	ISOLATED	ISOLATED
JOYFUL	JOYFUL	JOYFUL	JOYFUL	JOYFUL	JOYFUL	JOYFUL
ELATED	ELATED	ELATED	ELATED	ELATED	ELATED	ELATED
ENERGIZED	ENERGIZED	ENERGIZED	ENERGIZED	ENERGIZED	ENERGIZED	ENERGIZED
AGGRESSIVE	AGGRESSIVE	AGGRESSIVE	AGGRESSIVE	AGGRESSIVE	AGGRESSIVE	AGGRESSIVE
INSOMNIA	INSOMNIA	INSOMNIA	INSOMNIA	INSOMNIA	INSOMNIA	INSOMNIA

NOTES

MONDAY	TUESDAY	WEDNESDAY	THURSDAY	FRIDAY	SATURDAY	SUNDAY

W/C

MON	TUE	WED	THRS	FRIDAY	SAT	SUN
MOOD	MOOD	MOOD	MOOD	MOOD	MOOD	MOOD
☺	☺	☺	☺	☺	☺	☺
😐	😐	😐	😐	😐	😐	😐
🙁	🙁	🙁	🙁	🙁	🙁	🙁
WORRIED	WORRIED	WORRIED	WORRIED	WORRIED	WORRIED	WORRIED
TROUBLED	TROUBLED	TROUBLED	TROUBLED	TROUBLED	TROUBLED	TROUBLED
PANIC ATTACKS	PANIC ATTACKS	PANIC ATTACKS	PANIC ATTACKS	PANIC ATTACKS	PANIC ATTACKS	PANIC ATTACKS
SAD	SAD	SAD	SAD	SAD	SAD	SAD
FATIGUE	FATIGUE	FATIGUE	FATIGUE	FATIGUE	FATIGUE	FATIGUE
TEARFUL	TEARFUL	TEARFUL	TEARFUL	TEARFUL	TEARFUL	TEARFUL
TIRED	TIRED	TIRED	TIRED	TIRED	TIRED	TIRED
IRRITATED	IRRITATED	IRRITATED	IRRITATED	IRRITATED	IRRITATED	IRRITATED
HOPELESS	HOPELESS	HOPELESS	HOPELESS	HOPELESS	HOPELESS	HOPELESS
ISOLATED	ISOLATED	ISOLATED	ISOLATED	ISOLATED	ISOLATED	ISOLATED
JOYFUL	JOYFUL	JOYFUL	JOYFUL	JOYFUL	JOYFUL	JOYFUL
ELATED	ELATED	ELATED	ELATED	ELATED	ELATED	ELATED
ENERGIZED	ENERGIZED	ENERGIZED	ENERGIZED	ENERGIZED	ENERGIZED	ENERGIZED
AGGRESSIVE	AGGRESSIVE	AGGRESSIVE	AGGRESSIVE	AGGRESSIVE	AGGRESSIVE	AGGRESSIVE
INSOMNIA	INSOMNIA	INSOMNIA	INSOMNIA	INSOMNIA	INSOMNIA	INSOMNIA

NOTES

MONDAY	
TUESDAY	
WEDNESDAY	
THURSDAY	
FRIDAY	
SATURDAY	
SUNDAY	

W/C

MON	TUE	WED	THRS	FRIDAY	SAT	SUN
MOOD	MOOD	MOOD	MOOD	MOOD	MOOD	MOOD
☺ 🙂 😐	☺ 🙂 😐	☺ 🙂 😐	☺ 🙂 😐	☺ 🙂 😐	☺ 🙂 😐	☺ 🙂 😐
WORRIED	WORRIED	WORRIED	WORRIED	WORRIED	WORRIED	WORRIED
TROUBLED	TROUBLED	TROUBLED	TROUBLED	TROUBLED	TROUBLED	TROUBLED
PANIC ATTACKS	PANIC ATTACKS	PANIC ATTACKS	PANIC ATTACKS	PANIC ATTACKS	PANIC ATTACKS	PANIC ATTACKS
SAD	SAD	SAD	SAD	SAD	SAD	SAD
FATIGUE	FATIGUE	FATIGUE	FATIGUE	FATIGUE	FATIGUE	FATIGUE
TEARFUL	TEARFUL	TEARFUL	TEARFUL	TEARFUL	TEARFUL	TEARFUL
TIRED	TIRED	TIRED	TIRED	TIRED	TIRED	TIRED
IRRITATED	IRRITATED	IRRITATED	IRRITATED	IRRITATED	IRRITATED	IRRITATED
HOPELESS	HOPELESS	HOPELESS	HOPELESS	HOPELESS	HOPELESS	HOPELESS
ISOLATED	ISOLATED	ISOLATED	ISOLATED	ISOLATED	ISOLATED	ISOLATED
JOYFUL	JOYFUL	JOYFUL	JOYFUL	JOYFUL	JOYFUL	JOYFUL
ELATED	ELATED	ELATED	ELATED	ELATED	ELATED	ELATED
ENERGIZED	ENERGIZED	ENERGIZED	ENERGIZED	ENERGIZED	ENERGIZED	ENERGIZED
AGGRESSIVE	AGGRESSIVE	AGGRESSIVE	AGGRESSIVE	AGGRESSIVE	AGGRESSIVE	AGGRESSIVE
INSOMNIA	INSOMNIA	INSOMNIA	INSOMNIA	INSOMNIA	INSOMNIA	INSOMNIA

NOTES

MONDAY	
TUESDAY	
WEDNESDAY	
THURSDAY	
FRIDAY	
SATURDAY	
SUNDAY	

W/C

MON	TUE	WED	THRS	FRIDAY	SAT	SUN
MOOD	MOOD	MOOD	MOOD	MOOD	MOOD	MOOD
☺	☺	☺	☺	☺	☺	☺
😐	😐	😐	😐	😐	😐	😐
☹	☹	☹	☹	☹	☹	☹
WORRIED	WORRIED	WORRIED	WORRIED	WORRIED	WORRIED	WORRIED
TROUBLED	TROUBLED	TROUBLED	TROUBLED	TROUBLED	TROUBLED	TROUBLED
PANIC ATTACKS	PANIC ATTACKS	PANIC ATTACKS	PANIC ATTACKS	PANIC ATTACKS	PANIC ATTACKS	PANIC ATTACKS
SAD	SAD	SAD	SAD	SAD	SAD	SAD
FATIGUE	FATIGUE	FATIGUE	FATIGUE	FATIGUE	FATIGUE	FATIGUE
TEARFUL	TEARFUL	TEARFUL	TEARFUL	TEARFUL	TEARFUL	TEARFUL
TIRED	TIRED	TIRED	TIRED	TIRED	TIRED	TIRED
IRRITATED	IRRITATED	IRRITATED	IRRITATED	IRRITATED	IRRITATED	IRRITATED
HOPELESS	HOPELESS	HOPELESS	HOPELESS	HOPELESS	HOPELESS	HOPELESS
ISOLATED	ISOLATED	ISOLATED	ISOLATED	ISOLATED	ISOLATED	ISOLATED
JOYFUL	JOYFUL	JOYFUL	JOYFUL	JOYFUL	JOYFUL	JOYFUL
ELATED	ELATED	ELATED	ELATED	ELATED	ELATED	ELATED
ENERGIZED	ENERGIZED	ENERGIZED	ENERGIZED	ENERGIZED	ENERGIZED	ENERGIZED
AGGRESSIVE	AGGRESSIVE	AGGRESSIVE	AGGRESSIVE	AGGRESSIVE	AGGRESSIVE	AGGRESSIVE
INSOMNIA	INSOMNIA	INSOMNIA	INSOMNIA	INSOMNIA	INSOMNIA	INSOMNIA

NOTES

MONDAY	
TUESDAY	
WEDNESDAY	
THURSDAY	
FRIDAY	
SATURDAY	
SUNDAY	

W/C

MON	TUE	WED	THRS	FRIDAY	SAT	SUN
MOOD	MOOD	MOOD	MOOD	MOOD	MOOD	MOOD
☺ 😐 🙁	☺ 😐 🙁	☺ 😐 🙁	☺ 😐 🙁	☺ 😐 🙁	☺ 😐 🙁	☺ 😐 🙁
WORRIED	WORRIED	WORRIED	WORRIED	WORRIED	WORRIED	WORRIED
TROUBLED	TROUBLED	TROUBLED	TROUBLED	TROUBLED	TROUBLED	TROUBLED
PANIC ATTACKS	PANIC ATTACKS	PANIC ATTACKS	PANIC ATTACKS	PANIC ATTACKS	PANIC ATTACKS	PANIC ATTACKS
SAD	SAD	SAD	SAD	SAD	SAD	SAD
FATIGUE	FATIGUE	FATIGUE	FATIGUE	FATIGUE	FATIGUE	FATIGUE
TEARFUL	TEARFUL	TEARFUL	TEARFUL	TEARFUL	TEARFUL	TEARFUL
TIRED	TIRED	TIRED	TIRED	TIRED	TIRED	TIRED
IRRITATED	IRRITATED	IRRITATED	IRRITATED	IRRITATED	IRRITATED	IRRITATED
HOPELESS	HOPELESS	HOPELESS	HOPELESS	HOPELESS	HOPELESS	HOPELESS
ISOLATED	ISOLATED	ISOLATED	ISOLATED	ISOLATED	ISOLATED	ISOLATED
JOYFUL	JOYFUL	JOYFUL	JOYFUL	JOYFUL	JOYFUL	JOYFUL
ELATED	ELATED	ELATED	ELATED	ELATED	ELATED	ELATED
ENERGIZED	ENERGIZED	ENERGIZED	ENERGIZED	ENERGIZED	ENERGIZED	ENERGIZED
AGGRESSIVE	AGGRESSIVE	AGGRESSIVE	AGGRESSIVE	AGGRESSIVE	AGGRESSIVE	AGGRESSIVE
INSOMNIA	INSOMNIA	INSOMNIA	INSOMNIA	INSOMNIA	INSOMNIA	INSOMNIA

NOTES

MONDAY	
TUESDAY	
WEDNESDAY	
THURSDAY	
FRIDAY	
SATURDAY	
SUNDAY	

W/C

MON	TUE	WED	THRS	FRIDAY	SAT	SUN
MOOD	MOOD	MOOD	MOOD	MOOD	MOOD	MOOD
☺	☺	☺	☺	☺	☺	☺
😐	😐	😐	😐	😐	😐	😐
😕	😕	😕	😕	😕	😕	😕
WORRIED	WORRIED	WORRIED	WORRIED	WORRIED	WORRIED	WORRIED
TROUBLED	TROUBLED	TROUBLED	TROUBLED	TROUBLED	TROUBLED	TROUBLED
PANIC ATTACKS	PANIC ATTACKS	PANIC ATTACKS	PANIC ATTACKS	PANIC ATTACKS	PANIC ATTACKS	PANIC ATTACKS
SAD	SAD	SAD	SAD	SAD	SAD	SAD
FATIGUE	FATIGUE	FATIGUE	FATIGUE	FATIGUE	FATIGUE	FATIGUE
TEARFUL	TEARFUL	TEARFUL	TEARFUL	TEARFUL	TEARFUL	TEARFUL
TIRED	TIRED	TIRED	TIRED	TIRED	TIRED	TIRED
IRRITATED	IRRITATED	IRRITATED	IRRITATED	IRRITATED	IRRITATED	IRRITATED
HOPELESS	HOPELESS	HOPELESS	HOPELESS	HOPELESS	HOPELESS	HOPELESS
ISOLATED	ISOLATED	ISOLATED	ISOLATED	ISOLATED	ISOLATED	ISOLATED
JOYFUL	JOYFUL	JOYFUL	JOYFUL	JOYFUL	JOYFUL	JOYFUL
ELATED	ELATED	ELATED	ELATED	ELATED	ELATED	ELATED
ENERGIZED	ENERGIZED	ENERGIZED	ENERGIZED	ENERGIZED	ENERGIZED	ENERGIZED
AGGRESSIVE	AGGRESSIVE	AGGRESSIVE	AGGRESSIVE	AGGRESSIVE	AGGRESSIVE	AGGRESSIVE
INSOMNIA	INSOMNIA	INSOMNIA	INSOMNIA	INSOMNIA	INSOMNIA	INSOMNIA

NOTES

MONDAY	TUESDAY	WEDNESDAY	THURSDAY	FRIDAY	SATURDAY	SUNDAY

W/C

MON	TUE	WED	THRS	FRIDAY	SAT	SUN
MOOD	MOOD	MOOD	MOOD	MOOD	MOOD	MOOD
☺	☺	☺	☺	☺	☺	☺
😐	😐	😐	😐	😐	😐	😐
🙁	🙁	🙁	🙁	🙁	🙁	🙁
WORRIED	WORRIED	WORRIED	WORRIED	WORRIED	WORRIED	WORRIED
TROUBLED	TROUBLED	TROUBLED	TROUBLED	TROUBLED	TROUBLED	TROUBLED
PANIC ATTACKS	PANIC ATTACKS	PANIC ATTACKS	PANIC ATTACKS	PANIC ATTACKS	PANIC ATTACKS	PANIC ATTACKS
SAD	SAD	SAD	SAD	SAD	SAD	SAD
FATIGUE	FATIGUE	FATIGUE	FATIGUE	FATIGUE	FATIGUE	FATIGUE
TEARFUL	TEARFUL	TEARFUL	TEARFUL	TEARFUL	TEARFUL	TEARFUL
TIRED	TIRED	TIRED	TIRED	TIRED	TIRED	TIRED
IRRITATED	IRRITATED	IRRITATED	IRRITATED	IRRITATED	IRRITATED	IRRITATED
HOPELESS	HOPELESS	HOPELESS	HOPELESS	HOPELESS	HOPELESS	HOPELESS
ISOLATED	ISOLATED	ISOLATED	ISOLATED	ISOLATED	ISOLATED	ISOLATED
JOYFUL	JOYFUL	JOYFUL	JOYFUL	JOYFUL	JOYFUL	JOYFUL
ELATED	ELATED	ELATED	ELATED	ELATED	ELATED	ELATED
ENERGIZED	ENERGIZED	ENERGIZED	ENERGIZED	ENERGIZED	ENERGIZED	ENERGIZED
AGGRESSIVE	AGGRESSIVE	AGGRESSIVE	AGGRESSIVE	AGGRESSIVE	AGGRESSIVE	AGGRESSIVE
INSOMNIA	INSOMNIA	INSOMNIA	INSOMNIA	INSOMNIA	INSOMNIA	INSOMNIA

NOTES

MONDAY	
TUESDAY	
WEDNESDAY	
THURSDAY	
FRIDAY	
SATURDAY	
SUNDAY	

W/C

MON	TUE	WED	THRS	FRIDAY	SAT	SUN
MOOD	MOOD	MOOD	MOOD	MOOD	MOOD	MOOD
☺	☺	☺	☺	☺	☺	☺
😐	😐	😐	😐	😐	😐	😐
😟	😟	😟	😟	😟	😟	😟
WORRIED	WORRIED	WORRIED	WORRIED	WORRIED	WORRIED	WORRIED
TROUBLED	TROUBLED	TROUBLED	TROUBLED	TROUBLED	TROUBLED	TROUBLED
PANIC ATTACKS	PANIC ATTACKS	PANIC ATTACKS	PANIC ATTACKS	PANIC ATTACKS	PANIC ATTACKS	PANIC ATTACKS
SAD	SAD	SAD	SAD	SAD	SAD	SAD
FATIGUE	FATIGUE	FATIGUE	FATIGUE	FATIGUE	FATIGUE	FATIGUE
TEARFUL	TEARFUL	TEARFUL	TEARFUL	TEARFUL	TEARFUL	TEARFUL
TIRED	TIRED	TIRED	TIRED	TIRED	TIRED	TIRED
IRRITATED	IRRITATED	IRRITATED	IRRITATED	IRRITATED	IRRITATED	IRRITATED
HOPELESS	HOPELESS	HOPELESS	HOPELESS	HOPELESS	HOPELESS	HOPELESS
ISOLATED	ISOLATED	ISOLATED	ISOLATED	ISOLATED	ISOLATED	ISOLATED
JOYFUL	JOYFUL	JOYFUL	JOYFUL	JOYFUL	JOYFUL	JOYFUL
ELATED	ELATED	ELATED	ELATED	ELATED	ELATED	ELATED
ENERGIZED	ENERGIZED	ENERGIZED	ENERGIZED	ENERGIZED	ENERGIZED	ENERGIZED
AGGRESSIVE	AGGRESSIVE	AGGRESSIVE	AGGRESSIVE	AGGRESSIVE	AGGRESSIVE	AGGRESSIVE
INSOMNIA	INSOMNIA	INSOMNIA	INSOMNIA	INSOMNIA	INSOMNIA	INSOMNIA

NOTES

MONDAY	
TUESDAY	
WEDNESDAY	
THURSDAY	
FRIDAY	
SATURDAY	
SUNDAY	

W/C

MON	TUE	WED	THRS	FRIDAY	SAT	SUN
MOOD	MOOD	MOOD	MOOD	MOOD	MOOD	MOOD
☺ / 😐 / 🙁	☺ / 😐 / 🙁	☺ / 😐 / 🙁	☺ / 😐 / 🙁	☺ / 😐 / 🙁	☺ / 😐 / 🙁	☺ / 😐 / 🙁
WORRIED	WORRIED	WORRIED	WORRIED	WORRIED	WORRIED	WORRIED
TROUBLED	TROUBLED	TROUBLED	TROUBLED	TROUBLED	TROUBLED	TROUBLED
PANIC ATTACKS	PANIC ATTACKS	PANIC ATTACKS	PANIC ATTACKS	PANIC ATTACKS	PANIC ATTACKS	PANIC ATTACKS
SAD	SAD	SAD	SAD	SAD	SAD	SAD
FATIGUE	FATIGUE	FATIGUE	FATIGUE	FATIGUE	FATIGUE	FATIGUE
TEARFUL	TEARFUL	TEARFUL	TEARFUL	TEARFUL	TEARFUL	TEARFUL
TIRED	TIRED	TIRED	TIRED	TIRED	TIRED	TIRED
IRRITATED	IRRITATED	IRRITATED	IRRITATED	IRRITATED	IRRITATED	IRRITATED
HOPELESS	HOPELESS	HOPELESS	HOPELESS	HOPELESS	HOPELESS	HOPELESS
ISOLATED	ISOLATED	ISOLATED	ISOLATED	ISOLATED	ISOLATED	ISOLATED
JOYFUL	JOYFUL	JOYFUL	JOYFUL	JOYFUL	JOYFUL	JOYFUL
ELATED	ELATED	ELATED	ELATED	ELATED	ELATED	ELATED
ENERGIZED	ENERGIZED	ENERGIZED	ENERGIZED	ENERGIZED	ENERGIZED	ENERGIZED
AGGRESSIVE	AGGRESSIVE	AGGRESSIVE	AGGRESSIVE	AGGRESSIVE	AGGRESSIVE	AGGRESSIVE
INSOMNIA	INSOMNIA	INSOMNIA	INSOMNIA	INSOMNIA	INSOMNIA	INSOMNIA

NOTES

MONDAY	TUESDAY	WEDNESDAY	THURSDAY	FRIDAY	SATURDAY	SUNDAY

W/C

MON	TUE	WED	THRS	FRIDAY	SAT	SUN
MOOD	MOOD	MOOD	MOOD	MOOD	MOOD	MOOD
☺ ☹ 😐	☺ ☹ 😐	☺ ☹ 😐	☺ ☹ 😐	☺ ☹ 😐	☺ ☹ 😐	☺ ☹ 😐
WORRIED	WORRIED	WORRIED	WORRIED	WORRIED	WORRIED	WORRIED
TROUBLED	TROUBLED	TROUBLED	TROUBLED	TROUBLED	TROUBLED	TROUBLED
PANIC ATTACKS	PANIC ATTACKS	PANIC ATTACKS	PANIC ATTACKS	PANIC ATTACKS	PANIC ATTACKS	PANIC ATTACKS
SAD	SAD	SAD	SAD	SAD	SAD	SAD
FATIGUE	FATIGUE	FATIGUE	FATIGUE	FATIGUE	FATIGUE	FATIGUE
TEARFUL	TEARFUL	TEARFUL	TEARFUL	TEARFUL	TEARFUL	TEARFUL
TIRED	TIRED	TIRED	TIRED	TIRED	TIRED	TIRED
IRRITATED	IRRITATED	IRRITATED	IRRITATED	IRRITATED	IRRITATED	IRRITATED
HOPELESS	HOPELESS	HOPELESS	HOPELESS	HOPELESS	HOPELESS	HOPELESS
ISOLATED	ISOLATED	ISOLATED	ISOLATED	ISOLATED	ISOLATED	ISOLATED
JOYFUL	JOYFUL	JOYFUL	JOYFUL	JOYFUL	JOYFUL	JOYFUL
ELATED	ELATED	ELATED	ELATED	ELATED	ELATED	ELATED
ENERGIZED	ENERGIZED	ENERGIZED	ENERGIZED	ENERGIZED	ENERGIZED	ENERGIZED
AGGRESSIVE	AGGRESSIVE	AGGRESSIVE	AGGRESSIVE	AGGRESSIVE	AGGRESSIVE	AGGRESSIVE
INSOMNIA	INSOMNIA	INSOMNIA	INSOMNIA	INSOMNIA	INSOMNIA	INSOMNIA

NOTES

MONDAY	TUESDAY	WEDNESDAY	THURSDAY	FRIDAY	SATURDAY	SUNDAY

W/C

MON	TUE	WED	THRS	FRIDAY	SAT	SUN
MOOD	MOOD	MOOD	MOOD	MOOD	MOOD	MOOD
☺	☺	☺	☺	☺	☺	☺
😐	😐	😐	😐	😐	😐	😐
☹	☹	☹	☹	☹	☹	☹
WORRIED	WORRIED	WORRIED	WORRIED	WORRIED	WORRIED	WORRIED
TROUBLED	TROUBLED	TROUBLED	TROUBLED	TROUBLED	TROUBLED	TROUBLED
PANIC ATTACKS	PANIC ATTACKS	PANIC ATTACKS	PANIC ATTACKS	PANIC ATTACKS	PANIC ATTACKS	PANIC ATTACKS
SAD	SAD	SAD	SAD	SAD	SAD	SAD
FATIGUE	FATIGUE	FATIGUE	FATIGUE	FATIGUE	FATIGUE	FATIGUE
TEARFUL	TEARFUL	TEARFUL	TEARFUL	TEARFUL	TEARFUL	TEARFUL
TIRED	TIRED	TIRED	TIRED	TIRED	TIRED	TIRED
IRRITATED	IRRITATED	IRRITATED	IRRITATED	IRRITATED	IRRITATED	IRRITATED
HOPELESS	HOPELESS	HOPELESS	HOPELESS	HOPELESS	HOPELESS	HOPELESS
ISOLATED	ISOLATED	ISOLATED	ISOLATED	ISOLATED	ISOLATED	ISOLATED
JOYFUL	JOYFUL	JOYFUL	JOYFUL	JOYFUL	JOYFUL	JOYFUL
ELATED	ELATED	ELATED	ELATED	ELATED	ELATED	ELATED
ENERGIZED	ENERGIZED	ENERGIZED	ENERGIZED	ENERGIZED	ENERGIZED	ENERGIZED
AGGRESSIVE	AGGRESSIVE	AGGRESSIVE	AGGRESSIVE	AGGRESSIVE	AGGRESSIVE	AGGRESSIVE
INSOMNIA	INSOMNIA	INSOMNIA	INSOMNIA	INSOMNIA	INSOMNIA	INSOMNIA

NOTES

MONDAY	TUESDAY	WEDNESDAY	THURSDAY	FRIDAY	SATURDAY	SUNDAY

W/C

MON	TUE	WED	THRS	FRIDAY	SAT	SUN
MOOD	MOOD	MOOD	MOOD	MOOD	MOOD	MOOD
😊	😊	😊	😊	😊	😊	😊
WORRIED	WORRIED	WORRIED	WORRIED	WORRIED	WORRIED	WORRIED
TROUBLED	TROUBLED	TROUBLED	TROUBLED	TROUBLED	TROUBLED	TROUBLED
PANIC ATTACKS	PANIC ATTACKS	PANIC ATTACKS	PANIC ATTACKS	PANIC ATTACKS	PANIC ATTACKS	PANIC ATTACKS
SAD	SAD	SAD	SAD	SAD	SAD	SAD
FATIGUE	FATIGUE	FATIGUE	FATIGUE	FATIGUE	FATIGUE	FATIGUE
TEARFUL	TEARFUL	TEARFUL	TEARFUL	TEARFUL	TEARFUL	TEARFUL
TIRED	TIRED	TIRED	TIRED	TIRED	TIRED	TIRED
IRRITATED	IRRITATED	IRRITATED	IRRITATED	IRRITATED	IRRITATED	IRRITATED
HOPELESS	HOPELESS	HOPELESS	HOPELESS	HOPELESS	HOPELESS	HOPELESS
ISOLATED	ISOLATED	ISOLATED	ISOLATED	ISOLATED	ISOLATED	ISOLATED
JOYFUL	JOYFUL	JOYFUL	JOYFUL	JOYFUL	JOYFUL	JOYFUL
ELATED	ELATED	ELATED	ELATED	ELATED	ELATED	ELATED
ENERGIZED	ENERGIZED	ENERGIZED	ENERGIZED	ENERGIZED	ENERGIZED	ENERGIZED
AGGRESSIVE	AGGRESSIVE	AGGRESSIVE	AGGRESSIVE	AGGRESSIVE	AGGRESSIVE	AGGRESSIVE
INSOMNIA	INSOMNIA	INSOMNIA	INSOMNIA	INSOMNIA	INSOMNIA	INSOMNIA

NOTES

MONDAY	TUESDAY	WEDNESDAY	THURSDAY	FRIDAY	SATURDAY	SUNDAY

W/C

MON	TUE	WED	THRS	FRIDAY	SAT	SUN
MOOD	MOOD	MOOD	MOOD	MOOD	MOOD	MOOD
☺	☺	☺	☺	☺	☺	☺
😐	😐	😐	😐	😐	😐	😐
☹	☹	☹	☹	☹	☹	☹
WORRIED	WORRIED	WORRIED	WORRIED	WORRIED	WORRIED	WORRIED
TROUBLED	TROUBLED	TROUBLED	TROUBLED	TROUBLED	TROUBLED	TROUBLED
PANIC ATTACKS	PANIC ATTACKS	PANIC ATTACKS	PANIC ATTACKS	PANIC ATTACKS	PANIC ATTACKS	PANIC ATTACKS
SAD	SAD	SAD	SAD	SAD	SAD	SAD
FATIGUE	FATIGUE	FATIGUE	FATIGUE	FATIGUE	FATIGUE	FATIGUE
TEARFUL	TEARFUL	TEARFUL	TEARFUL	TEARFUL	TEARFUL	TEARFUL
TIRED	TIRED	TIRED	TIRED	TIRED	TIRED	TIRED
IRRITATED	IRRITATED	IRRITATED	IRRITATED	IRRITATED	IRRITATED	IRRITATED
HOPELESS	HOPELESS	HOPELESS	HOPELESS	HOPELESS	HOPELESS	HOPELESS
ISOLATED	ISOLATED	ISOLATED	ISOLATED	ISOLATED	ISOLATED	ISOLATED
JOYFUL	JOYFUL	JOYFUL	JOYFUL	JOYFUL	JOYFUL	JOYFUL
ELATED	ELATED	ELATED	ELATED	ELATED	ELATED	ELATED
ENERGIZED	ENERGIZED	ENERGIZED	ENERGIZED	ENERGIZED	ENERGIZED	ENERGIZED
AGGRESSIVE	AGGRESSIVE	AGGRESSIVE	AGGRESSIVE	AGGRESSIVE	AGGRESSIVE	AGGRESSIVE
INSOMNIA	INSOMNIA	INSOMNIA	INSOMNIA	INSOMNIA	INSOMNIA	INSOMNIA

NOTES

MONDAY	TUESDAY	WEDNESDAY	THURSDAY	FRIDAY	SATURDAY	SUNDAY

MEDICATION TRACKER

Medicine List

#	Medicine	Dose	Start Date	End Date	Frequency

Tracker

#	Medicine	Dose	Date	Time	Notes

MEDICATION TRACKER

Medicine List

#	Medicine	Dose	Start Date	End Date	Frequency

Tracker

#	Medicine	Dose	Date	Time	Notes

MEDICATION TRACKER

Medicine List

#	Medicine	Dose	Start Date	End Date	Frequency

Tracker

#	Medicine	Dose	Date	Time	Notes

MEDICATION TRACKER

Medicine List

#	Medicine	Dose	Start Date	End Date	Frequency

Tracker

#	Medicine	Dose	Date	Time	Notes

MEDICATION TRACKER

Medicine List

#	Medicine	Dose	Start Date	End Date	Frequency

Tracker

#	Medicine	Dose	Date	Time	Notes

MEDICATION TRACKER

Medicine List

#	Medicine	Dose	Start Date	End Date	Frequency

Tracker

#	Medicine	Dose	Date	Time	Notes

MEDICATION TRACKER

Medicine List

#	Medicine	Dose	Start Date	End Date	Frequency

Tracker

#	Medicine	Dose	Date	Time	Notes

MEDICATION TRACKER

Medicine List

#	Medicine	Dose	Start Date	End Date	Frequency

Tracker

#	Medicine	Dose	Date	Time	Notes

MEDICATION TRACKER

Medicine List

#	Medicine	Dose	Start Date	End Date	Frequency

Tracker

#	Medicine	Dose	Date	Time	Notes

MEDICATION TRACKER

Medicine List

#	Medicine	Dose	Start Date	End Date	Frequency

Tracker

#	Medicine	Dose	Date	Time	Notes

Use this section to document your day, express your feelings freely, write down notes, things to remember anything that will help you to feel better.

SAFETY PLAN

Early warning signs that a crisis may be happening (thoughts, images, behavior, mood)

_____

_____

_____

Things that I can do to distract me from my problems

_____

_____

_____

Internal coping strategies which I can use (prayer, play my games console, affirming quote or mantra)

_____

_____

_____

People I can call for help (name & numbers)

_____

_____

_____

Professionals I can call for help

_____

_____

_____

Things I need to do to make my environment safe

_____

_____

_____

Two reasons for being alive

1. _____

2. _____

Made in the USA
San Bernardino, CA
06 May 2018